Sew Much Fun

14 Projects to Stitch & Machine Embroider

C&T PUBLISHING

© 2002 by Oklahoma Embroidery Supply & Design

Developmental Editors: Barb Kuhn, Carolyn Aune

Technical Editor: Carolyn Aune

Copy Editor: Lucy Grijalva

Cover Designer: Kristen Yenche

Book Designer: Kristen Yenche

Illustrator: Kirstie L. McCormick

Production Assistant: Kirstie L. McCormick

Photography: Christy Burcham/OESD, Kirstie L. McCormick/C&T Publishing

Published by C&T Publishing, Inc., P.O. Box 1456, Lafayette, California 94549

Front and Back Cover Photography: Kirstie L. McCormick

Attention Teachers: C&T Publishing, Inc. encourages you to use this book as a text for teaching. Contact us at 800-284-1114 or www.ctpub.com for more information about the C&T Teachers Program.

Library of Congress Cataloging-in-Publication Data

Sew much fun: 14 projects to stitch & embroider / Oklahoma Embroidery Supply & Design.

        p. cm.

    ISBN 1-57120-180-7

    1. Embroidery, Machine--Patterns. I. Oklahoma Embroidery Supply & Design.

TT772 .S48 2002

746.44--dc21

                                        2002005470

Printed in China

10 9 8 7 6 5 4 3 2 1